# A Weekend with Nanny and Pa:
*Memories of Lincolnton, Georgia and
Clarks Hill Lake in the 1980s*

## DANA PUTNAM BURKHART

For Doris Patton "Nanny" Poston, the memory maker

For Wade, my first friend and playmate

For George, my partner in creating the next generation of memories

For Mom & Dad, the storytellers and providers of creative space to explore

For Josie, Roper, & Ramsey, the recipients of my memories

In Memory of William Joseph "Pa" Poston

**THE LITTLE RIVER BRIDGE**

*The Little River Bridge is a gateway to a magical world
of childhood joy and simplicity.
I used to hold my breath as we drove over it, but now I breathe it in
and try to hold on to the Good Ole Days.*

Special Thanks to Chenille Williams and Lara Sadowski

Text and illustrations copyright © 2016 Dana Putnam Burkhart
All rights reserved.
ISBN-10: 0692676627
ISBN-13: 978-0692676622

Library of Congress Control Number: 2016913879

## ABOUT THIS BOOK

While contemplating the idea of time travel and reliving moments from my past, one of my heart's loudest and most immediate requests was to relive a typical weekend with my grandparents, Nanny and Pa Poston, at their lake house in Lincolnton, Georgia, in the 1980s. The lake "house," a modified trailer, was near Clarks Hill Lake (which was later renamed Thurmond Lake). It was not on the water, and conditions were Spartan at best. We made our own fun and enjoyed the simplest of pleasures. The time travel idea arose and flitted away like a song or a sunset.

Years later, I learned my brother Wade had purchased a lake house in the same neighborhood in Lincolnton, and my eyes unexpectedly welled with tears. Wade indicated his desire to recreate our childhood memories for his children, and forgotten emotion bubbled to the top of my soul. I decided to recreate our childhood memories for my daughter and his children by writing and illustrating this book.

I thank God for the ability to eat the food, smell the aromas, see the sights, catch the fish, bang the pots and pans, and curl up in that rocking chair one more time. I hope you are inspired to pull your loved ones closer for a spell and travel with us back to the dirt roads and wooden docks of Clarks Hill Lake.

"We are almost there," says Mama as she drives Doodlebug and her brother over the Little River Bridge to the lake house at Indian Cove.

Doodlebug feels the wind from Mama's car lift her hand in flight,

and her heart races with excitement looking forward to the days and nights ahead.

When Mama's car pulls into the driveway, Nanny and Pa are standing in the front yard with outstretched arms waiting to hug Doodlebug and her brother Little Charlie.

Since they arrived at the lake house earlier in the day, Nanny and Pa have relaxed, and now they are ready to make some weekend memories!

It's Friday night, so Nanny and Pa load Doodlebug and Little Charlie into Pa's van to go to dinner at their favorite restaurant, the Swamp Guinea.

Pa's van has a picture of his dog Pug on the wheel cover.
Everyone at the lake knows Nanny and Pa.

After dinner, Pa unfolds the sofa bed for Doodlebug and Little Charlie.

They would be sad at the sight of their beds at home, but here at the lake house, Doodlebug and Little Charlie know that the night still holds a lot of fun!

Pa settles down in his favorite chair with Pug curled up in his lap.

Nanny invites Doodlebug to rock with her in the creaky rocking chair. They hug each other tightly for more than fifty rocks and two lullabies.

Nanny sighs, "You are getting so big, Doodlebug! You won't always want to rock with your Old Nanny."

"Yes, I will!" Doodlebug energetically replies.

Doodlebug and Little Charlie turn into "monkeys jumping on the bed" while commercials play between their favorite television shows.

As they catch their breath from a rambunctious pillow fight, they realize their bellies ache from laughing so hard.

Little Charlie remembers the most fun he's ever had on the sofa bed.

He and Doodlebug watched a street party on television and waited for a giant ball of lights to slide down a pole. When the ball got to the bottom, the lights flashed "1-9-8-3." Fireworks popped and blazed, and everyone cheered, hugged, and kissed!

At the lake house, when the ball of lights got to the bottom of the pole, Little Charlie and Doodlebug banged Nanny's pots and pans with wooden spoons while Pa kissed Nanny for good luck.

Little Charlie's thoughts snap back to the present, and he asks, "When will we bang on the pots and pans again?"

Pa says, "It's almost Fall. New Year's Eve will be here before we know it!"

After watching Doodlebug and Little Charlie roughhouse on the sofa bed and enjoy all their favorite shows, Nanny tucks them under the covers with soft kisses. Little Charlie falls asleep right away, but Doodlebug keeps watching the television set in front of her.

Pa's deep voice interrupts the scary intro music of the late late show, "You are a little night owl!  You keep me up late every Friday night watching this old stuff!"

Doodle thinks to herself, "I'm scared!  You are keeping *ME* awake!"

Doodlebug offers only one argument aloud, "Nooooo, Pa! You are the *real* night owl!"

In the morning, Doodlebug and Little Charlie wake to the wonderful smell of bacon sizzling on the stove in the kitchen behind their bed.  Doodlebug tiptoes to the edge of the counter and quietly sneaks a perfect piece of crispy, salty bacon.

Just as Doodlebug holds her breath
and returns to the bacon plate in hopes of another slice,
she is startled by Pa's cheery voice,

"Why, there goes the *Bacon Snatcher*!"

Later, Nanny gets very hot working in her beautiful garden in the yard behind the lake house.

After spending many weekends planting, weeding, and watering, she finally picks tomatoes, squash, and zucchini.

Pa is very proud of the bounty from Nanny's garden.  Even though he didn't help with the planting, fertilizing, and harvesting, Pa drives Little Charlie in the golf cart down the red dirt road to take Nanny's best vegetables to the neighbors.  Mr. George's house is the first stop.

"Here is a basket of the best squash, zucchini, and tomatoes around!" exclaims Pa.

"I'm a lucky bachelor," replies Mr. George, "when Mrs. Pat isn't sending me a warm plate, she sends these!  Please send her my love, Mr. Bill!"

Next, Pa lets Little Charlie guide the golf cart wheel further down the red dirt road as they take the rest of Nanny's vegetables to Mr. Jimmy's house.

Pa parks the golf cart.

"Me and Little Charlie have some of Pat's prizes from the garden for you!" Pa beams.

"Many thanks, Bill! We will enjoy 'em," Mr. Jimmy replies.

"Where is Doodlebug?" asks Mr. Jimmy's daughter, Nancy.

"Back at the lake house with her Nanny," replies Pa.

Nancy's brother Jay and Little Charlie run off to play in the woods while Pa talks with Mr. Jimmy. Little Charlie and Jay listen in the distance.

"Do you think the Corps of Engineers will let us have some water in the lake this year?" Pa asks Mr. Jimmy.

We just pray for rain to keep it full," Mr. Jimmy replies.

Little Charlie looks up from his game with Jay and exclaims, "I thought engineers drove trains!"

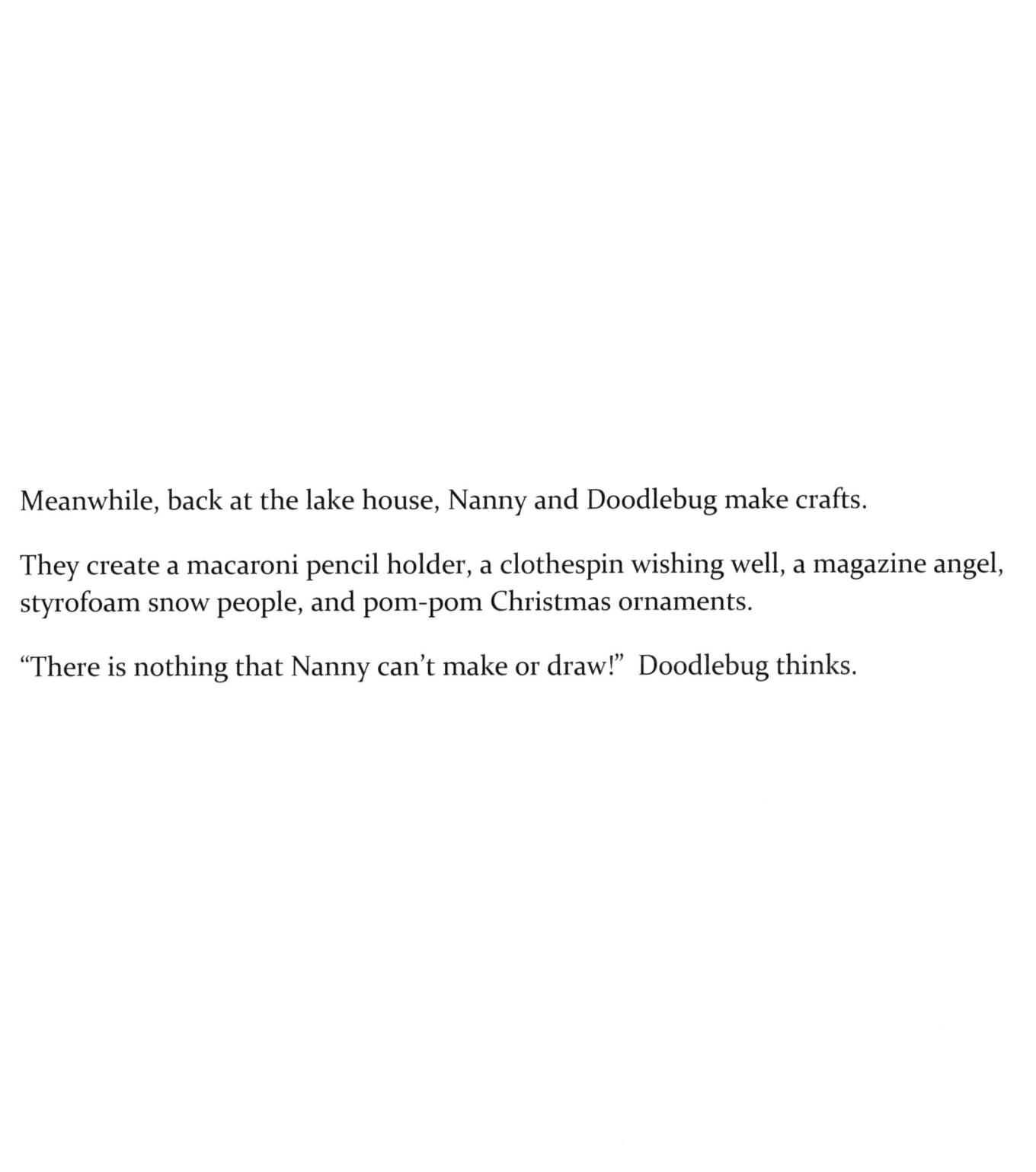

Meanwhile, back at the lake house, Nanny and Doodlebug make crafts.

They create a macaroni pencil holder, a clothespin wishing well, a magazine angel, styrofoam snow people, and pom-pom Christmas ornaments.

"There is nothing that Nanny can't make or draw!" Doodlebug thinks.

After Pa and Little Charlie return to the lake house, the neighbors Mr. and Mrs. Fox drop by for a visit.

Rusty and Ilsa, their German Shepherds, stand vigil just outside the screen door as Mr. Fox pinches Little Charlie's nose.

Mrs. Fox fills Nanny in on all the neighbors' plans, comings and goings, and everything that happened since last weekend. As the conversation winds down, Mrs. Fox exclaims, "See you at church tomorrow!"

After Nanny, Doodlebug, and Little Charlie step back inside the lake house, the screen door slams behind them. "You gals!" Pa exclaims, "Your mouths just *run* like an old bell-clapper!"

That night, Pa makes steak,
and Nanny makes her special homemade french fries for dinner.

Little Charlie says the blessing,

*"God is great, God is good.
Let us thank Him for our food.
By His hands, we all are fed.
Give us Lord, our daily bread."*

"That was a long prayer, Little Charlie! You must not be very hungry!" smiles Pa.

Little Charlie and Doodlebug are thankful for the tasty food they enjoy every weekend with Nanny and Pa.

The next morning, Pa drops Nanny, Doodlebug, and Little Charlie off at Double Branches, the little country church down the road.

Doodlebug loves the sound of Nanny's voice singing, "In the Sweet By and By," and she sings along, too. Doodlebug enjoys reading along in the old hymnal. Its cover is frayed, and it smells like a library.

In the parking lot after the service, everyone says "time flies" and that Doodle and Little Charlie are growing *so* fast!

Doodlebug doesn't feel like she is growing *that* fast. Time moves so slowly while she is sitting in the church pew trying to understand the preacher and his long sermons.

On the way back from church,
Doodlebug sees Price's Store out the window of Pa's van.

"Let's go in!" she chirps.

Filled with excitement, Doodlebug and Little Charlie rush to the counter to look at the candy display.

"You can each pick five pieces!" Nanny calls out from the back of the store.

"This is probably the last place in the world that has penny candy," Pa adds as he hands the cashier a tiny shiny dime.

Everyone piles back into Pa's van. After driving silently for a while, Pa unexpectedly swerves into L.W.'s Bait Shop.

Before he gets out of the van, Pa turns around and looks at Doodle and Little Charlie over his shoulder, "I need a haircut, and L.W. can fix me right up!"

"There are no gas stations that have restaurants, barbershops, and fish bait at home," says Doodlebug.

"That's because you don't live in the country!" replies Pa.

Inside the building, L.W. brushes off the back of the red barber chair and Pa sits down.

"Hellooooo Billy!" L.W. exclaims as he buttons a plastic drape around Pa's neck.

"I just need shaping up," Pa says.

L.W. combs down Pa's hair, which grows long on one side.

"Tee hee! Bah ha ha haa!" Doodlebug and Little Charlie giggle behind their hands.

L.W. is the only person that doesn't make Pa angry by combing down his hair.

After Pa's haircut, everyone returns to the lake house.
Little Charlie and Doodlebug change clothes and get ready to go fishing.
They dig for worms in the backyard with Nanny.

"Here are some wiggly old night crawlers!" Nanny exclaims as she shovels the worms into an old coffee can with some dirt.

On the dock at the end of the dirt road, Nanny, Pa, Doodlebug, and Little Charlie wait for their red and white bobbers to go underwater.

When Doodlebug's bobber goes under, her fishing pole bends over. Nanny and Pa call out directions, "Reel 'em in! Reel! Reel in the fish!"

"I hate waiting for the fish to bite," exclaims Little Charlie after the excitement dies down, "but I sure do love catching fish!"

Nanny, Pa, Doodlebug, and Little Charlie catch nine bream total.  The fish flip, flap, and flop as Doodlebug pulls the fish basket out of the water to prepare to pack up.

"Not bad for a late Sunday afternoon!" booms Pa.

Nanny takes a photo with her flash bulb camera, and she turns the dial to advance the film.

On the way back to the lake house, Pa blows the golf cart horn in celebration of a great catch. "Oooga! Oooga!"

Nanny sets up a folding table between the lake house and Mr. and Mrs. Fox's house and covers it with newspaper. Then she cleans the fish scales and bones away.

"Pee Ewwwww!" Doodlebug exclaims while fanning her nose from the fishy smell.

"Aren't you glad your Nanny is so tough, Doodlebug?" Pa taunts, "How would you like to scale the fish? *I* sure am glad she's tough!"

Pa rolls the fish in corn breading and fries them in the peanut oil cooker for a delicious fresh meal.

After dinner, Doodle and Little Charlie pack their suitcases, and Pa and Nanny begin the long drive back home.

Doodlebug listens to the wind whistle as Pa cracks the window near the rear view mirror. She shivers from a slight chill in the evening air. Doodlebug tugs Little Charlie to the back window of Pa's van, and they watch the Little River Bridge grow longer behind them.

When Doodlebug and Little Charlie get home, Doodlebug sits at the kitchen table and lets out a long sigh. She stares into space with sad eyes.

Little Charlie slides into the seat next to her and breaks the silence. "The weekend will be here again soon!" he cheers.

"Yes, Little Charlie," agrees Doodlebug as a smile creeps across her face, "another weekend with Nanny and Pa will be here before we know it!"

The end.

www.ingramcontent.com/pod-product-compliance
Lightning Source LLC
LaVergne TN
LVHW072054070426
835508LV00002B/96